MOODS OF
NORTHUMBERLAND
National Park

TONY HOPKINS

HALSGROVE

First published in Great Britain in 2004

Title page photograph: *Female fox-moth.*

British Library Cataloguing-in-Publication Data
A CIP record for this title is available from the British Library

ISBN 1 84114 372 3

HALSGROVE
Halsgrove House
Lower Moor Way
Tiverton, Devon EX16 6SS
Tel: 01884 243242
Fax: 01884 243325
email: sales@halsgrove.com
website: www.halsgrove.com

Printed and bound by Oriental Press

INTRODUCTION

Of all the National Parks of England and Wales, Northumberland is the most remote and the least visited, a place of far horizons and frontier memories. Its boundary was drawn up in the 1950s to create as much fresh air as possible for people weary of austerity and worried about the Cold War.

In the north, the Park includes the Cheviot massif, a landscape for exhilarating walks, open grasslands and deep valleys radiating from high rounded hills. The middle section of the Park includes the heather moors of Harbottle and Simonside, and the Rede and North Tyne Valleys, infamous for centuries as the refuge of moss-troopers and reivers. To the west is the Border Forest Park, and to the south lie waves of moorgrass prairie and the Whin Sill, along which runs Hadrian's Wall, one of the most important archaeological features in Europe.

Altogether, the National Park covers an area of nearly four hundred square miles, most of it empty space, as close to the elements and to nature as you can get in an overstressed country at the start of the twenty-first century.

Sir Walter Scott enjoyed the spirit of the Northumberland hills and what is now the National Park: 'I like the very nakedness of the land, it has something bold and stern and solitary about it.' But Scott was also drawn by the hint of danger, the stories of conflict and the ruins of lost civilizations. Until the last century, few travellers ventured north of the Wall: 'Vipers and serpents innumerable, with all other kinds of wild beasts, infest that place...' Now we wish that the wildlife had not been so thoroughly subdued, and we conjure ghosts from weathered stones.

This book is a personal selection of images drawn from a landscape I have grown to care deeply about over a period of nearly twenty-five years. But of all the landscapes I know it is the most difficult to photograph, the most capricious, the hardest to pin down.

It is always better to see things yourself rather than to rely on the words or pictures of anyone else. So although I believe some of my photographs come close to catching the spirit of Northumberland, I hope the main effect of this book will be to encourage a few more people to explore the place for themselves. But not too many people.

Tony Hopkins

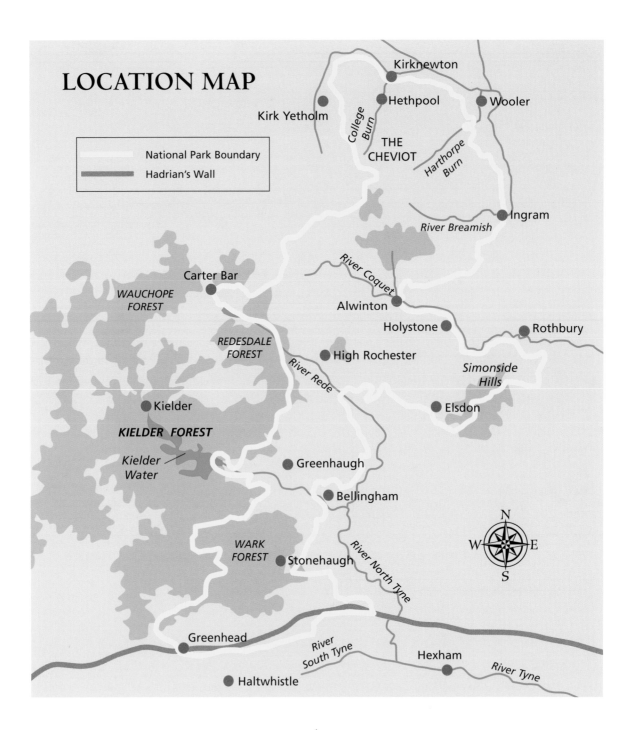

The summit of Shill Moor, with tussocks of moorgrass flattened against a bitter north-west wind. In the distance is the 2676ft (815m) whaleback of The Cheviot.

West Hill, on the north-west shoulder of Cheviot. Hang-gliders sometimes use the upper slope of this elegant hill as a launch-pad, harnessing the west wind and the updraught of air. On clear days it is usually over West Hill that the first wisps of cloud form, pirouetting and shape-shifting as they blot out the sun.

Midwinter monochrome: heather and snow across the Cheviot massif,
from Monday Cleugh and Gains Law, south-west to Hedgehope and Cheviot.

The College Valley from Hethpool Bell.
The two hills on the west flank of the valley are Great Hetha and Sinkside: both are topped by Iron-Age hillforts.

The last patch of morning sunshine racing across the College Valley, picking out
the russet of early-frosted bracken and the wet roof of Hethpool pele-tower.

College Burn and the slopes of Hare Law, looking beyond the
rainbow to Hethpool Bell and the Collingwood Oaks.

A path to the Henhole,
a remote hanging valley
at the head of the
College Burn.

A flock of sheep grazing beside the College Burn (mid left of picture), look like antelope lost in the vastness of the Ngorongoro Crater. It comes as a surprise to see an English landscape transformed in scale into an apparent wilderness. But like the Ngorongoro, the Cheviots were created by volcanic action: a few thousand years ago aurocks and elks would have grazed these 'haughlands.'

Cairn Hill and the final ascent to the summit of Cheviot. The terrain is worse than it looks – a thick bed of waterlogged peat, so walking can be a weary business. The stone slabs are a recent godsend, making it possible even in a wet winter to reach Northumberland's highest point.

Dusk over King's Seat, on the Cheviot Border ridge.

Hambleton Hill, from the hillfort looking east over Wooler, a gateway settlement to the northern National Park.

Hawsen Crags, between Cold Law and Black Seat, with the Harthope
Valley in deep shadow in the background. Looking east towards the coast.

Housey Crags, one of the most elegant of the hardened andesite tors, on the steep climb
between the Harthope Valley and Hedgehope (second highest summit in the Cheviots).

Snow and ice on the wind-scoured slopes of Hedgehope, looking north to The Cheviot.

Greenside and Hartside Farms – in
the Breamish Valley looking towards
Linhope and Ritto Hill.

Linhope Spout after heavy autumn rain. The rock outcropping beside the waterfall is granite, a hard crystalline rock forming the inner core of the Cheviots.

Frost-scorched bracken and the wooded cleugh of Dunmoor Burn, on the south-east slope of Hedgehope, just above Linhope.

Tussocks of moorgrass below Cushat Law. The word 'cushat' means wood pigeon, though the habitat here seems completely unsuitable. This is pipit and curlew country, until you reach the dark green depth of Kidland Forest, to the top left of the picture.

Late September along the Breamish Valley, at the foot of Ewe Hill and with Blackface sheep grazing the north bank of the river. The purple 'glidders' or scree in the background is too steep and unstable for most plants to gain a root-hold.

The River Breamish, looking west to Bulby's Wood. The boulders in the river here are used as fishing pitches by dippers, on the lookout for minnows and stonefly larvae.

June along the Harthope Burn near Langlee. A colourful time of year, with bell-heather in flower on the slopes of Pinkie Shank.

The Breamish Valley, from Brough Law over the tree-bowered hamlet of Ingram towards the coast.

Half way down the path from Brough Law. Snow-clouds building from the north-east.

Above:
Skyline tors at the head of the Harthope Valley:
Housey Crags, with the smaller Langlee Crags to the left.

Right:
A clear, cloudless day, perfect for a winter walk. The view east,
towards Langlee Crags, from the ridge-crest in the previous picture.

Autumn dawn: the sun
rising through early mist.

Snout End and Ritto Hill, in the upper Breamish Valley. Looking north to Hedgehope.

Cunyan Crags, one of the most prominent landscape features on the skyline of the Breamish Valley. The rock is andesite, baked and metamorphosed because it was close to a granite intrusion 390 million years ago.

Cairn on the slopes of Hogdon Law. Piles of stone may seem transient elements of the landscape, but many were gathered in prehistory, their meaning or purpose long forgotten.

Bleached grasslands sweeping east from Hare Law to Roddam Burn.

An emerald-green island in a russet sea: inbye pasture, reclaimed from the hill and improved by lime and fertilizers. The Dod from Heddon Hill, near Ilderton.

Stormy weather as splintered sunshine picks out interlocking hill shanks in the Upper Coquet Valley.

A low cloud ceiling on a diamond-bright morning, looking
north-east over Shorthope Hill to Uswayford and The Cheviot.

Suckler cattle, north of the Coquet Valley. In the background is the Carshope Plantation and Thirl Moor.

South from Barrow Law, over Barrowburn and Wedder Leap, with the silver thread of the River Coquet shining in the winter shadows. Cheviot and Swaledale x sheep graze the rough pasture.

Frosty morning on Barrow Law.

The Border Ridge (Scotland to
the right and in the distance):
from Windy Gyle to Mozie Law.

The Coquet in spring, at
Barrow Scroggs near Alwinton.

The Simonside Hills, looking south from Cartington, over Thropton and the green valley of Coquetdale, to the forested sandstone ridge of Simonside. The tors or low pinnacles along the treeless ridge-crest are prehistoric cairns or beacons.

November sunshine and Jacob sheep: Rothbury in Coquetdale, south-west to Tosson and the Simonside.

Rothbury from the south bank of the River Coquet. All Saints' church is mainly Victorian but with original thirteenth-century features. The heather-covered ridge in the background, topped by a prehistoric hillfort, is known as Rothbury Terraces.

Weathered outcrops of Fell Sandstone are a feature of the Rothbury area.
Some of the larger rocks, like this one on Garleigh Moor, are worth a closer look...

The sandstone outcrop on Garleigh Moor, from another angle, looking north to Simonside.
The surface of the main rock is patterned by cup and ring marks, engraved or incised during the Bronze Age.
Today rock art like this is a mystery, although when it was created it must have had a clear and obvious purpose.

The path to Spylaw: south
over Grain Sike, with Coldrife
on the skyline.

A heft of sheep, grazing the heather moorland of Caudhole Moss, south of Dove's Crag in the Simonside Hills.
The heather is strip-burned to provide plenty of young growth to feed grouse.
In the misty distance, to the south-west, is the edge of Harwood Forest.

Above:
Garleigh Moor and Cragside, north-east to the coast, from the Simonside ridge. Garleigh is one of the most important prehistoric landscapes in the National Park, with ancient field systems and settlements, burials and rock art sites. In the mid-right of the picture are the ramparts of Lordenshaws Iron Age hillfort.

Left:
Rothbury and Coquetdale, looking north from the Simonside ridge.

Dark tussock moth, a speciality of Northumberland's heather moors.

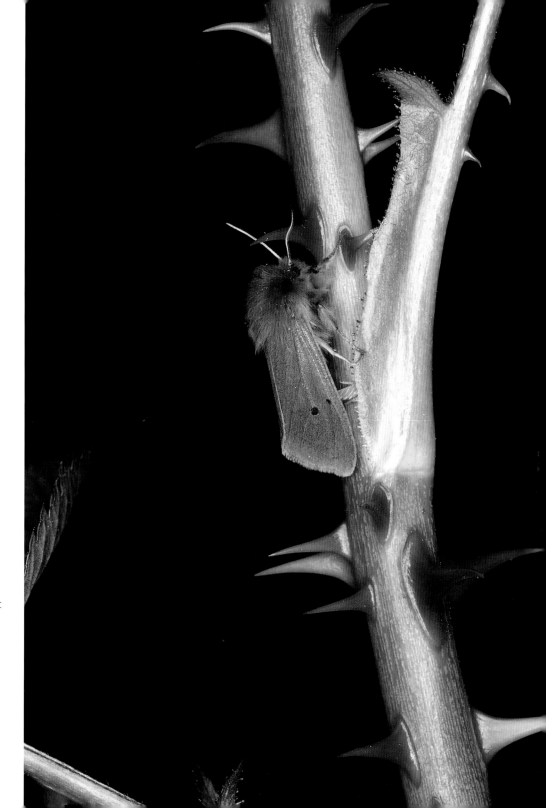

Ruby tiger moth: one of the prettiest
of the smaller moorland moths.

Northern eggar moth: one of the biggest British insects. This is a female moth freshly emerged from a cocoon hidden among the heather. The male is more often seen by walkers, because it flies by day.

Female emperor moth, freshly emerged from her cocoon and sitting quietly in a heather clump to 'call' for a mate. She emits a scent which wafts far and wide, attracting males.

Harbottle, from the path to the Drake Stone. In the mid-left of the picture is the motte or grassy hill of Harbottle Castle.

Harbottle Castle, a strategic stronghold and home of the Lords of Redesdale in the Border Wars.
Most of the stonework has been spirited away to be re-used in local halls and houses.
What remains has been conserved by the National Park Authority.

Mist over the sandstone crags of Whitfield Hill.

The Harbottle Hills in early autumn: heather and bracken-beds on a gusty bright morning.

Above:
Elsdon, from the pinfold across the town green to the medieval church, with the vicar's pele-tower behind. The common space once contained a gallows, pillory and cockpit, and was used for fairs and markets as well as for a midsummer bonfire.

Left:
Meanders of the River Coquet, east from Harehaugh and Hepple.

Early frost: the gateway and track to Midgy Ha'.

St Cuthbert's church in Elsdon. This medieval church, sometimes called the 'Cathedral of the Rede', was where the dead from the Battle of Otterburn were buried in 1388.

Midwinter half-light, and the sky threatening more snow: Houx Hill looking south towards Byrness and Redesdale Forest.

Snow-drifts on the upper slopes of Byrness Hill, looking west to Catcleugh and Carter Fell.

Snow-laden spruce and larch
trees in Redesdale Forest.

Catcleugh Reservoir and part of the Border Forest Park. A patchwork of conifers,
lost in the snowy waste of Redesdale, seen from the lower slopes of Byrness Hill.

Above:
Heather in full bloom: the sight and scent can be irresistible, especially for bees.

Right:
Northumberland's heather moors turn vivid mauve for a few weeks every August.

Cowberry growing among heather on the Simonside Hills.

Red grouse, the main consumer of fresh heather shoots on the managed moors.

Peat pools and the Potter Burn, looking north-west over a sweep of moor-grass towards Padon Hill.

The pepperpot monument on the top of Padon Hill, looking east towards Otterburn. The bell-shaped structure was erected in the 1920s, but most of the unworked stones were already here. Padon (or Peden) was a roving Presbyterian preacher in the seventeenth century, in the dark days of repression when congregations were obliged to worship in secret, sometimes on hilltops. Each stone carried up the hill was an act of defiance, and over the years the resulting cairn would have been visible for miles around.

The Dargues Valley and Troughend Common, from Padon Hill looking south-east.

Wet and featureless moorland, once called the Waste, looking west to Broadsike, with the edge of Kielder Forest in the right background. Once a place of treachery and conflict, it was the territory of reivers and outlaws.

Grazing into the wind: a cut of Swaledale sheep south of Gibshiel, on the flank of Great Dodd.

A penful of blue-faced Leicester tups. Their aloof, intellectual expressions are not a reflection of their true nature.

Blackface ewe lambs at an autumn market.

Mottle-faced Mule lambs: a popular cross between blue-faced Leicester tups and Blackface ewes.

Left:
Hareshaw Dene footpath,
one of the best flowery places
in the National Park.

Right:
Hareshaw Linn, the beautiful
waterfall at the end of the
dene – a short walk from
Bellingham. In spring and early
summer the path verges on
the way to the linn are covered
with primrose, dog-violet,
sanicle and cow-wheat.

Autumn oak canopy, near Hesleyside in the North Tyne Valley.

Drystone walls and a rowan, on the edge of a heather bank in early September. The rowan's berries only last a few days, and the leaves are among the first to fall or be scattered by strengthening autumn winds.

Billsmoor Park, an ancient deer park enclosing attractive woodland (and a few deer), in the Grasslees Valley north of Elsdon.

East across the Grasslees Valley, from Billsmoor Park up steep bracken slopes and old enclosures to the blacklands and crags of Miller's Moss and Whitfield Hill. A fallow deer is grazing among the rushes.

Melancholy thistle: a tall spineless species with big shaving–brush flower-heads
common in the North Tyne Valley and along road verges around Kielder.

A century ago Falstone was a village in a wilderness, on a railway line to nowhere: a settlement based around a farm and pele-tower and the site of an Anglo-Saxon cross. Now it nestles in the shadow of Kielder Dam and the edge of Kielder Forest and the Border Forest Park. The railway closed in the 1960s and road traffic passes Falstone by. It is still a quiet village, but in a different kind of wilderness.

Looking north-east across the North Tyne Valley to Mount Pleasant, below the forest plantations of Green Eyes Crags.

The North Tyne Valley, looking west towards the Border Forest Park. Most of the planting
for the forest took place in the 1950s. Farms and shepherds' cottages bought by the
Forestry Commission were allowed to decay, to disappear into the shadows.

Above:
Midsummer along the North Tyne at Ridley Stokoe.
Alders and willows shade the deep pools of this famous salmon river.

Left:
Hoar frost and mist on the river: the North Tyne
at its confluence with the Chirdon Burn.

Meadowsweet crowds the edge of a hay-meadow, along the North Tyne Valley near Camp Cottage.

Early purple orchid on
a Northumberland road verge.

Gatehouse Bastle, near Greenhaugh. In the darkest days of Border unrest farm communities had to protect themselves and their stock against reiving Scots. When an attack was expected, families herded their best animals into the bastle, climbed into the upper room through a trapdoor and pulled up the ladder after them. With no windows and five-foot thick walls, bastles were either a safe refuge or a death trap.

A ruined bastle in a forest clearing at Sidwood. Most bastle-houses date back to the late sixteenth century.

Most fortified farmhouses or border bastles were built to the same design and measured about thirty five feet by twenty five. With such thick walls the living space must have been cramped. So when peace came to the Borders farmers were quick to build better houses, often within yards of their old bastles, as in this example at Horneystead, above the Warks Burn.

Roadside sign at Horneystead (as it is spelled on maps). The huntsman is either blowing his horn or finishing his Percy Special (a traditional pre-hunt snifter of whisky and cherry-brandy).

Autumn at Lowstead, on the banks of the Blacka Burn.
The farmhouse and the barn to the left are converted bastles, built in the sixteenth century.

The valley of the Warks Burn, looking west to Windy Edge.

Footpath east from Crookbank, on the banks of the Warks Burn at Stonehaugh.

Warks Burn from Stonehaugh, looking north-east to Standingstone Clints.

Hexham, in the Tyne Valley, is the most important gateway town to Hadrian's Wall and the National Park. The medieval core of the town is clustered around the moot hall, gaol and abbey, all visible in this view from Fell Side.

Hexham Abbey from the Sele. The original church, dedicated to St Andrew, was built from Roman stone. Features of the impressive seventh-century structure still survive, notably the crypt, but most of the present building dates back to the twelfth century and later.

The track from Burn Divot, across a treacherous mire in the windswept country north of Hadrian's Wall.
Place-names in this part of the National Park are wonderfully evocative: Moss Peterel,
Watch Hill, Hangingshields, Scotchcoultard, Wileysike and Farglow.

The ruins of Burn Divot. Miles from your nearest neighbour: peat to burn, nothing to do
but gather your sheep and listen to the wind. No wonder nobody has lived here for half a century.

North of Hadrian's Wall: across Greenlee Lough to the Whin Sill, from Highshields Crags to Steel Rigg. A barbarian's-eye view of the edge of the Roman Empire.

Galloway cow and blue-grey calf. A tough breed, suited to the cold climate of the Wall country and gaining in popularity again because the meat is leaner than that of continental breeds.

Cotton-grass, one of the characteristic plants of Northumberland's famous mires. The seed-heads appear in the middle of summer, and in autumn the leaves turn rich russet.

Heath spotted orchid, found on acid soils and dry moorland.

Above:
Round-leaved sundew. The sticky pin-cushion leaves catch
insects, providing the plant with essential nutrients.

Right:
Bog violet, growing on a bed of moss in a shady peat-puddle.

Meadow brown butterfly. Still a common sight in pastures and meadows throughout the National Park.

Large heath butterfly. A speciality of the Border mires, on the wing in late June and early July. Cross-leaved heath is a favourite nectar-source. The eggs are laid on cotton-grass.

Golden-ringed dragonfly. A green-eyed monster: the biggest British dragonfly.
A scarce species, but found around several of the Border mires. This one was photographed at Sidwood.

Elephant hawk-moth. Elegant and beautiful, and common now that its foodplant, rosebay willowherb, is widespread. On the wing in June, when it visits the flowers of honeysuckle and campion.

Lapwing nest. Like most wading birds, the lapwing lays four speckled eggs and relies on camouflage to make them invisible to potential predators. Walk away from a nest for a few paces, then turn back and try to find it again: not easy!

Snipe nest. Again, impossible to find except by nearly treading on a sitting bird.

A cold bright day, looking east to Hotbank from the low pastures north of the Wall.

Cattle on the White Bank, looking north-west over Caw Lough and West Hotbank to the distant ridge of Winshields.

Birches on a crystal morning.
Archers Wood near Sewingshields.

The long snowy track to Moralee, north from *Brocolitia*.
The only footprints are those of a hungry rabbit.

Above:
Damp, misty and drizzly weather. North of Sewingshields.

Right:
Heavy cloud about to spoil the early sunshine: the view
east over Little Shield from near Grandy's Knowe.

Late-summer sunrise: from Windshields Crags east to Crag Lough and Steel Rigg.

Mist in the Tyne Valley, looking south-east from Hadrian's Wall near Cuddy's Crags.

Midsummer haze: Barcombe Fell and High Shield Farm, south from Highshield Crags.

Grey dolerite: worn teeth on the north face of the Whin Sill, Sewingshields Crags.

Sunrise over Hadrian's Wall,
from Peel Crags.

Warm colours bathing the south face of Hadrian's Wall, on a cold October morning with the grass bleached and the clouds threatening rain.

Dove Crag and Sewingshields Crags, from King's Wicket. The line of Hadrian's Wall is occupied here by an ordinary drystone wall, though the stone is certainly original.

Hadrian's Wall: the descent
from Cuddy's Crags eastwards,
with Housesteads Crags
in the distance.

A clear day looking westwards into Cumbria from Walltown Crags. This is one of the best and easiest sections of Hadrian's Wall to visit, a five minute walk from a car park and very photogenic, even in a drought.

A view the other way, along the Nine Nicks at Walltown Crags.

Along the crest of the Whin Sill. The path crosses the stile to stay with the line of Hadrian's Wall, right to left.

Rapishaw Gap, where the Pennine Way strikes north from Hadrian's Wall, across Ridley Common and into Wark Forest.

Housesteads Roman Fort. Built on the dip slope of the Whin Sill, but set against Hadrian's Wall so its north face runs along the cliff-top. In the background is Grindon Lough, which marks the southern boundary of the National Park.

Vindolanda Roman Fort, north of Bardon Mill and a mile south of Hadrian's Wall. *Vindolanda* was originally built to defend the Stanegate but was later incorporated into the Wall system. Some outstanding archaeological finds have been made here, including the famous writing tablets, and there are ongoing digs every year. The adjacent museum is excellent too.

Stonework of Thirlwall Castle, near Greenhead. The medieval tower-house
was constructed entirely from stone 'quarried' from nearby Hadrian's Wall.

The ruins of Thirlwall Castle, after conservation work by the National Park Authority.

Causeway House, along the road to *Vindolanda* and one of the few surviving examples of heather-thatch anywhere in England. The windows are typical of Northumberland vernacular style – solid, square and functional.

Breakfast-time at Walltown. Sheep have to work hard to find suitable grazing
on the rushy pasture south of the Wall. Windshields Crags in the distance.

Above:
The Mare and Foal: the remaining standing stones of a prehistoric stone circle,
close to Shield on the Wall and the Military Road: looking west into the sunset.

Right:
After an hour's drive and an hour's climb in the dark: the dawn was clear,
but then clouds appeared from nowhere. Twenty minutes after sunrise, with
one photograph taken, it was impossible to tell whether the world would
be bathed in sunshine or drowned in heavy rain. It was the rain.

Sunset over Grindon Lough.